Second Glances
An Introduction to Seeing

Ann Lauwers

DEDICATION

To all those who've seen and felt the presence of Nature's spirits, but thought they were crazy for doing so.

The Story Behind the Images of Second Glances

After months of preparation for my son's wedding in my back yard, I was welcoming the following days to spend in Tawas with my family where we would celebrate a family reunion. Tawas City is a small retirement town on the east side of the state of Michigan.

As a photographer you learn to grab every opportunity you can to take pictures. The sun rises over Lake Huron, giving the bay a new canvas of color each morning. When it was mentioned that I wanted to go out to Tawas Point State Park to take pictures of the sunrise, my sisters were quick to chime in that they wanted to go as well. So long as I provided them with coffee, of course. The next morning we got up extra early, coffee in hand and headed out to the park. In the dark, we walked the beach anxiously waiting for the sun to come up, searching for that perfect spot to capture the morning's rays. We chatted like the little girls we once were as I set up my camera & tripod. It's funny how siblings can be all grown up with families of their own and yet as soon as we see each other, we immediately assume the roles we had as children. Our smiles and laughter were showing how much we had missed it.

As the sun came up over the bay, I got the shots I had hoped for. "Just another beautiful sunrise in Tawas" the locals would say. An occurrence you never get tired of.

It had been years since we visited the park so we weren't in any hurry to leave. We strolled along the beach with our feet in the water, picking up our morning's treasures of shells and driftwood. As I watched the waves wash up on the beach, I noticed the designs they were making. Some say the blue color in the sand is the polluting oils from the cargo ships passing by. Maybe it is, but from an artist point of view, the blue oil, the brown and tan sand, and the white froth from the waves were making a great contribution to that morning's design. Seizing my opportunity, I took several shots before moving along in search of the next great design.

Like all great vacations, they come to an end and we go back to our everyday lives with hopes and plans to do it again. It was now time to get back to work. After saving the wedding and family pictures, all that was left were those great sand design images. I put one up full screen and sat there enjoying the flow of color and texture. Then it happened. I began to see something else. A face. Then two. These sand designs where now looking back at me with wonderful fantasy filled expressions. Once this happens, you can't just ignore it. They're there, plain as day. My mind tried to go back to when I didn't see them so I could just enjoy the design but I could. I wrestled with questions, "Were those faces really there? Why didn't I see them when I was taking the pictures? I had spent at least five minutes photographing them, surely I should have seen it then. Is this why I liked it so much, the faces and the fantasy? Am I making this up? Am I nuts?"

I once read that our eyes see much more than our minds can comprehend at one time. The design was changing with every wave. Surely there wasn't enough time to study it. I then began to use a darkroom technique of dodging and burning (lightening and darkening) on the image in small areas so others could see what was appearing to me. At that moment "Wave Spirits" was born and the game of finding Nature's spirits began.

The game isn't as easy as it seems. Inspired by my find, I began searching daily for faces, but that didn't work. I've learned to just photograph the designs and textures whenever they appear and take a closer look later. Using my artistic eye, I search for patterns that nature put there herself. Patterns in the dirt after a rain, the formation of bark on a tree, or even the swirls the wind makes on a crust of snow are perfect places to look. Often I'm pleasantly surprised to find them right in plain sight such as with "Happy Rocks". Happy Rocks were right there in my garden for years before I discovered them. I had walked past them every day on my way to the mailbox. They weren't hiding, they were just there waiting for me to see them.

I once heard it said, "If you don't know something exists, then you will never see it." I believe that now, being taught the simple lesson of seeing.

The following pages contain just a few of Nature's spirits I've been blessed to photograph.

If you keep your eyes open and your heart filled with wonder, the magic will appear.

Ann

IMAGE NAMES

Wave Spirits as it first appeared on the beach. Here you can see the blue oil that was washing up on shore.

Wave Spirits

What Does the Mountain Have to Say?

Mountain Man appeared at Yellowstone National Park, Wyoming.

At Mammoth Hot Springs, water rises through the limestone, carrying high amounts of dissolved calcium carbonate. At the surface, carbon dioxide is released and calcium carbonate is deposited. This forms travertine, the chalky white rock of the terraces. Due to the rapid rate of deposition, these features constantly and quickly change making them great subjects for photography.

I see a man with a butch haircut and a microphone held up under his nose as if to address his audience.

Fort Yellowstone, Yellowstone National Park, Wyoming

If this formation has been there since 1872, then surely it has been entertained over the passing years. The guy on the bottom left seems to be covering his eye or holding his forehead as if to say "Oh my, did you see that?"

Totem of Faces

Wandering Spirit

I was photographing this driveway looking for the best way to show how it bends and loving the way the sun was shining through the trees. I was pleasantly surprised later when I noticed I actually had company.

If you look just right of the large tree on the left, I make out a ghost lady floating just above the pile of rocks. My belief in ghost has expanded to watching for them not just in the night but any time of the day.

This image has not been altered in any way.

Fountain Lady

Fountain Lady at Longwood Gardens Conservatory, Pennsylvania

We were visiting the gardens when I photographed this wonderful fountain. It was intended to be used as a reference shot for a fountain I wanted in my own garden at home.

Fountain Lady stands with her face looking up to the sky, her chest out, arms down to her sides, and her left knee bent slightly.

This image has not been altered in any way.

Bear Story

I love studying this paving stone. I'm always compelled to come up with a children's story about a bear looking back over his shoulder, a small creature on his back, and a fish swimming alongside them.

This image has not been altered in any way.

Paver Stone Story

Paving stones are wonderful story tellers. This bear is carrying her cub in her mouth while walking alongside a river. Their reflection shows in the water. I felt an Indian story emerging.

This image has not been altered in any way.

Amazing is the only way to describe *Water Fairies*.

My mom was driving when I suddenly made her stop the car for another one of those quick picture moments. As I stood on the bridge looking over the shallow river, the colors were begging my attention.

On the left are shadows from the trees above making faces, The fallen leaves create fairies on the creek floor. On the right bottom corner appeared a face who's expression looks to be one of a quiet hello.

Water Fairies

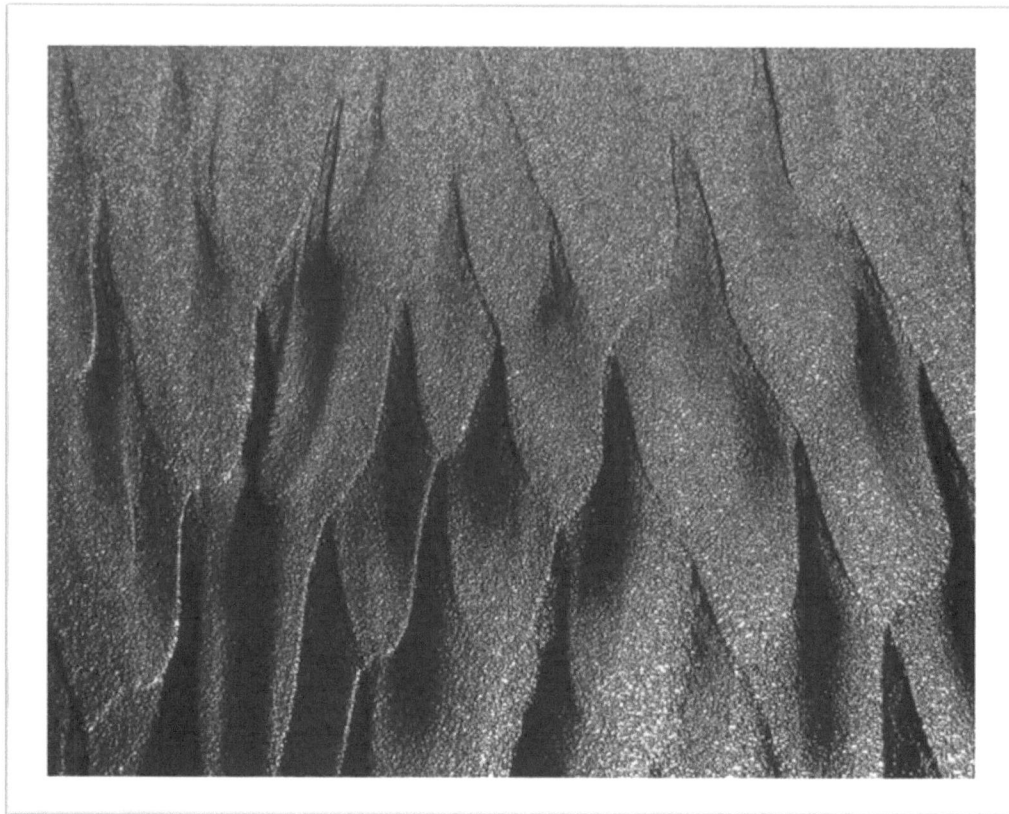

The sands on the beach of Surfer's Paradise, Australia seems so different than the sand I'm used to in Michigan. The waves from the South Pacific Ocean are so powerful the designs in the sands change in a matter of seconds. I was lucky enough to capture *Sands of Geese* before the under-tow took me.

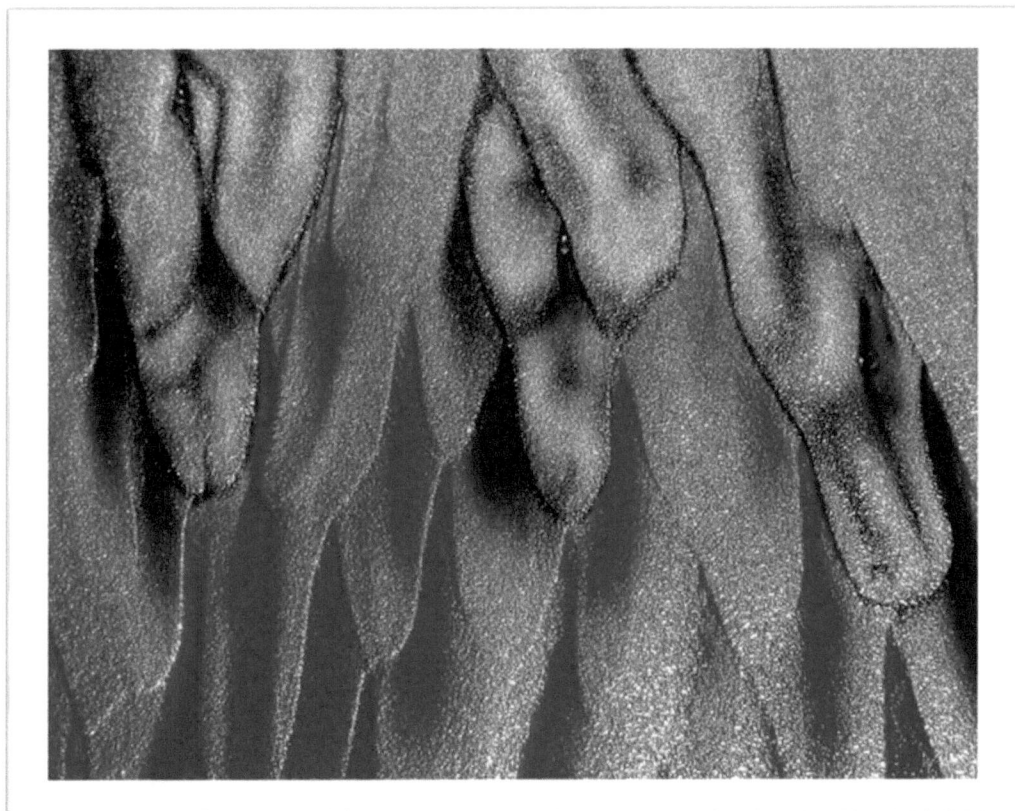

Sands of Geese

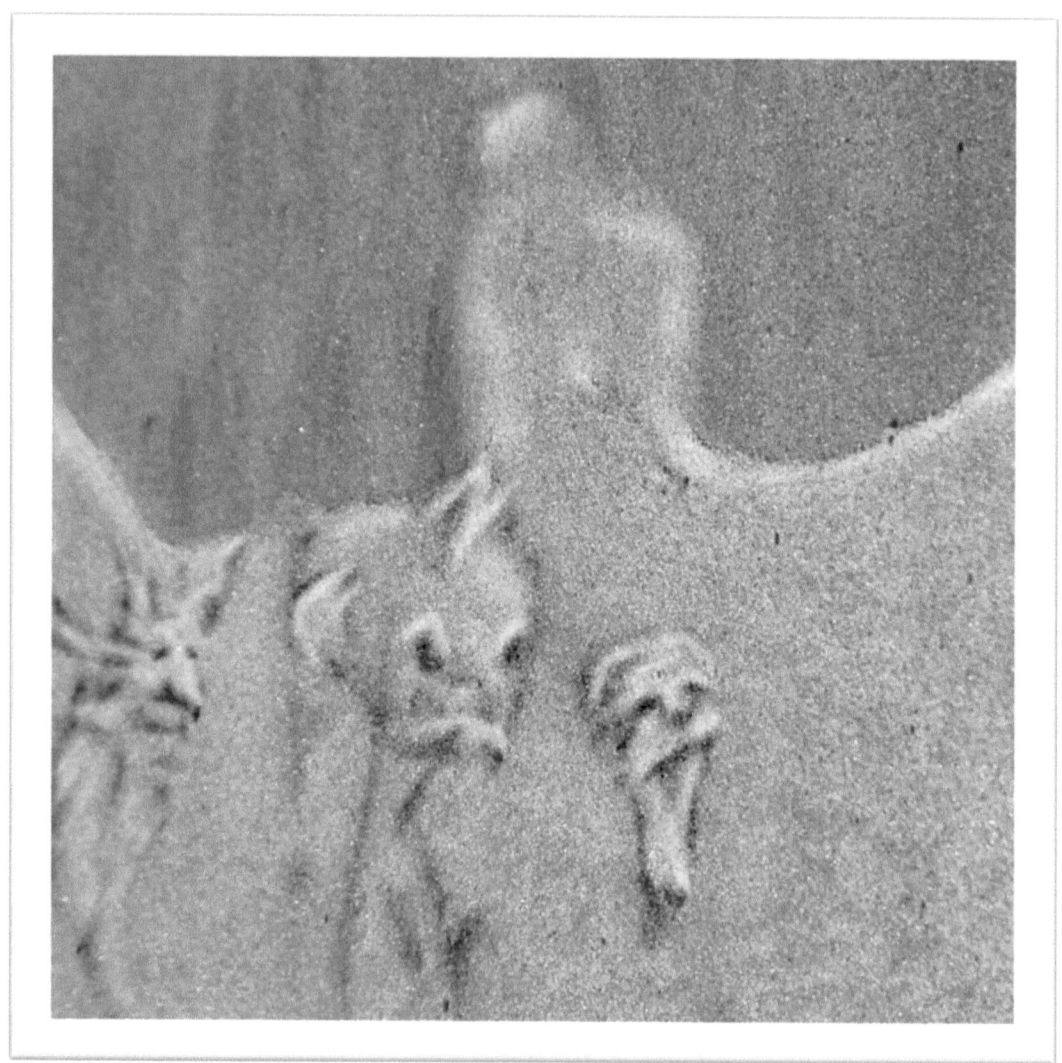

Sand Spirits

Sand Spirits were found on the beach of Lexington Michigan.

I'm beginning to understand how the sands of different beaches have a personality of their own.

Rose Nose

I spend a lot of time in my gardens, not just planting and weeding, but sitting in amazement of the different forms and colors of each plant.

Duck Head

Blue Water Spirits came from the algae growing on the bottom of the thermal stream in Thermopolis, Wyoming.

Blue Water Spirits

Water Nixie was laying at the bottom of a hot spring in Yellowstone National Park, Wyoming.

She seems to be blowing a kiss to the little nixie she is holding in her hand, as little fairies watch on.

Water Nixies

Sand Dragon

Sand Dragon was found on the beach of East Tawas, Michigan.

Do you see an animal head in the sand? I see a dragon, but others have seen a horse or a dog. What do you see?

Indian Chief

Indian Chief tree bark was another design that was in my garden.

He didn't stay long. As the tree grew, the bark expanded and merged into other designs. We enjoyed his presence while he visited.

Fiery Duck

At the campfire one night it was decided to do an experiment and take several shots randomly to see what I would get. Now I wonder if this is why people enjoy staring into a fire. Is the fire giving us a constant array of images so fast that our minds just don't have time to register them?

Fiery Scream

Stump Story

Do you see them now? To me, this tree stump resembles a dragon embracing it's young.

What do you see?

Tree Gremlins

Tree Gremlins is truly one of my favorites.

Have you ever wondered what stories the trees could tell?

Happy Rocks

Are you enjoying the game?

I hope this book has awakened your inner child and inspired you to get out in nature and take that second glance.

About the Author

As a lifelong artist, Ann has honed her abilities to see the world through an artistic lens. Her attention to detail, composition and color has won her several awards locally and nationally for her photographic retouching.

Her own company, An Artist View Photography, was conceived as an outlet for her creative passions through which she has won awards within her home state of Michigan.

Ann's endless curiosity and her love of nature makes everyday a creative venture. Whether it's the beauty of a single rose, or helping others see a face in a tree, she uses that artistic lens to show the world what they may have missed.

These prints and more are available by visiting Ann's website;
www.AnArtistView.net

www.ingramcontent.com/pod-product-compliance
Lightning Source LLC
Chambersburg PA
CBHW041512280526

45792CB00004B/1224